Pop Pop's House

Written By

Eboni Joi Creighton

Illustrated By

Tracey Taylor Arvidson

AuthorHouse™
1663 Liberty Drive
Bloomington, IN 47403
www.authorhouse.com
Phone: 1 (800) 839-8640

Published by AuthorHouse 03/07/2019

ISBN: 978-1-5462-7886-3 (sc)
ISBN: 978-1-5462-7887-0 (e)

Library of Congress Control Number: 2019901425

Print information available on the last page.

Any people depicted in stock imagery provided by Getty Images are models,
and such images are being used for illustrative purposes only.
Certain stock imagery © Getty Images.

This book is printed on acid-free paper.

Because of the dynamic nature of the Internet, any web addresses or links contained in this book may have changed
since publication and may no longer be valid. The views expressed in this work are solely those of the author and do not
necessarily reflect the views of the publisher, and the publisher hereby disclaims any responsibility for them.

authorHOUSE®

Pop Pop's House

This book is dedicated to all the Pop Pops
who share love and wisdom,
as much as hugs and cookies.

To my father,
Theodore R. White.

Thank you for exposing me to the arts and encouraging every creative
idea. For every crayon, for every piece of paper,
for that big fat elephant over there,
for EVERYTHING-
I love you Daddy!

At my Pop Pop's House, there are LIGHTBULBS, SCREWS, and TOOLS . . . IMPORTANT MACHINES AND T^INGS.

My Pop Pop can FIX ANYTHING!

At my Granddaddy's House,

there's always something that needs a fixin'.
I ride shotgun to the orange Hardware Store.
I drive the car cart all **WILLY NILLY** while he
gets the goods. We never leave without our
secret hotdog and chips.

2

A wrench
Screw
drivers
Old FlatHead Philip
Nuts -n- bolts
A 'wideamower'
Workbench thingamajigs
Even my Daddy can't fix 'tings'
as good as you
You're my strong Pop Pop
and
I LOVE YOU!

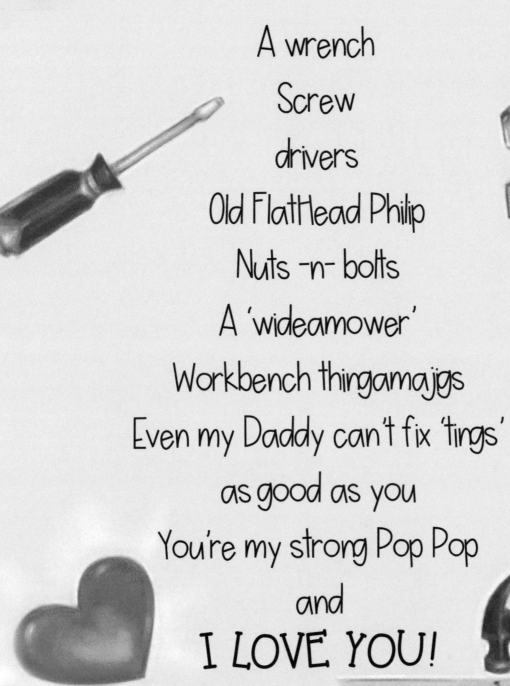

3

At my Pop Pop's House,

there are CAREGIVERS and WHEELCHAIRS.

There are other Grandpas and Grandmas but none as special as mine.

4

My Pop Pop and me,
we like to watch movies,
eat Mickey D's and ice-cream.
We have Tea Parties.
We play cars and puzzles.
We jam to all kinds of music.

Sometimes my Pop Pop
FORGETS
what he was saying.
But he ALWAYS REMEMBERS
to HUG and KISS ME!

POP POP SAYS
Give me some
SUGAH
He even calls me
PUDDIN'
Do you think it's because
I'M SO SWEET?

MY PAPA calls me SON

Even though I'm his GRANDSON

It's okay, I like it that way.

MY GRANDDADDY calls me BUD

because I'm his BUDDY

MY GRANDPA calls me SPORT

I wonder if it's because
I'm SO short?

At my Papa's House, there's always BBQ. SMOKEY KISSES greet us at the door. If you are lucky enough to get a taster off the GRILL, you better not drop it!

Barefoot in the grass

RIBS

No plates

Mason Jar Cucumbers

Vinegar + Salt

DILL PICKLES

UUUUUMPH.

MAKES HAIR GROW ON YOUR CHEST!

At my Pops' House, there is a LAKE.

Pops sits on the patio with his crossword and coffee.

The nights are long and peaceful.
I tiptoe out of sight when I hear Pops and the
Old-timers talk about grown-up stuff. I think he sees
me but he lets me listen anyways.

ZOOOOOMMMMMM

We FLY across the LAKE

I'M DAYDREAM'N

WE'RE FISH-N'

Silent Conversations

Fried Fish for dinner
We will MAKE!

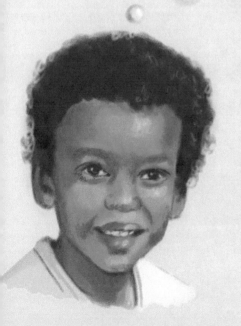

CHOCOLATE Milk
Cookies & TREATS
GALORE!

My Grandpa SPOILS me to pieces
NO WONDER IT'S HIM THAT I
ADORE!

At my Pop Pop's House, there are long lazy afternoon naps in a RECLINING CHAIR.
While his belly climbs

UP

AND

DOWN

I pretend he is a great

BiG CUDDLY BEAR!

NAP NAP

Sleep Tight

MY PAPA BEAR

Hold me Tight

{SNORE}

[snore]

15

At my Grandpa's House,
life is totally SWEET.
I get to eat all my favorite cereals. I can pour and
pour all the way up to the top!

My Grandpa will never ever tell me to stop!

LUCKY ME

I'm his Lucky Charm
Loops-n-Fruits
All Day Long
Into the **MAGICAL MILK** they
JUMP

So SUGARY
So SWEET
Puffs and Pebbles, Cocoas and Fruits
We go together
Like Cereal & Milk
MY SWEET GRANDPA AND ME

At my Papa's House, there is a BIG Kid Bike
so RED so SHINEY, so NEW.

There is always an adventure
and a laugh or two!

MY Papa

is

KING

He lives in a castle and treats me like a

QUEEN!

At my Grandpa's House, there are lots of
PEPPERMINTS.
I can have as MANY as I want.
Mommy
says
that's
why

the
dog
has
NO TEETH!

21

At my Paw Paw's House, there's a farmhouse and barn. We milk the cows and fetch the eggs. We catch fireflies then drink lemonade. Summer Fun at Paw Paw's means fried green tomatoes and homegrown jam.

Porch SWINGING
Grass CHEWING
LAYING in the shade
Tractor Rides
Handkerchiefs
No tissue
PRICKLEY KISSES
Dandelion Wishes
Berry PICKN'
Finger LICKN'
Just good ol' country livin'
With my easy-going PAW PAW

At my Grandfather's House, there are crossword puzzles, peanuts in the shell, and polka dot bananas. There's soul music playing on the tape recorder. My Grandfather takes me wherever he goes. Just my Grandfather and me and an armful of dollies.

24

SMILE, Say hello.

Put it back where you found it.

Say please.

Stand Tall.

Tuck your shirt in

Pull up your britches

That skirt's too short

Be brave

Look it up in the Dictionary

One day you will be smarter than me

Dress for success

Speak Up! I can't hear you!

Say Thank You.

Smile, You're BEAUTIFUL.

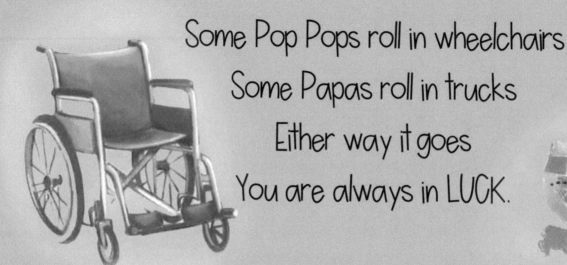

Some Pop Pops roll in wheelchairs
Some Papas roll in trucks
Either way it goes
You are always in LUCK.

Some Pop Pops live near
And some live far
Maybe your Grandpa lives with you?

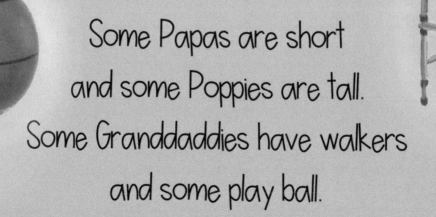

Some Papas are short
and some Poppies are tall.
Some Granddaddies have walkers
and some play ball.

Perhaps Grandpa likes to snooze
in his relaxing chair.

No matter what kind of Grandpa it is,
they all care.

WHAT KIND OF POP POP
DO YOU HAVE?

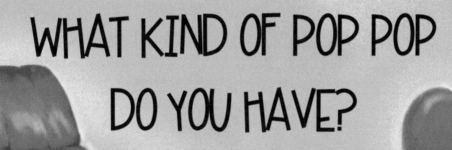

Printed in the United States
By Bookmasters